NATIONAL GEOGRAPHIC

D0503626

Ladders

THE CHESAPEAKE BAY

Read to find out about the resources of the Chesapeake.

The CHES
on a Skipjack

by Barbara Keeler

The Chesapeake Bay covers more than 11,600 square kilometers (4,480 square miles). That is more area than the state of Delaware.

PENNSYLVANIA
Susquehanna R.
MARYLAND
Port of Baltimore
Baltimore
Potomac R.
Washington, D.C.
NEW JERSEY
DELAWARE
Rappahannock R.
Chesapeake Bay
VIRGINIA
ATLANTIC OCEAN
James R.
York R.

0   50   100 Miles
0   50   100 Kilometers

N W E S

Welcome to the Chesapeake Bay. We are about to board a sailboat called a skipjack for a cruise of the Chesapeake. What's so special about a trip aboard a skipjack, you may ask? Well, skipjacks are old-style working boats that have sailed on the Chesapeake for over 200 years. They were important fishing boats, once used to dredge, or dig, along the bottom of the Bay for oysters. Today motorboats have replaced most skipjacks, so sailing on a skipjack is something like taking a trip back in time.

A skipjack races across the Bay's waters. Wind in the boat's sails moves it swiftly forward.

As we set sail and begin to discover the Bay, don't forget to look up and feel one of the Bay's most abundant **natural resources:** moving air, or the wind! The wind fills the skipjack's sails and easily drives the boat through the waves and across the Bay. In the distance you may spot sailboats racing each other. Watch closely. As they churn through the water, they may try to steal each other's wind. To steal wind, one boat will pull alongside another boat and get in between the wind and the other boat's sail. This blocks the wind from entering the second boat's sail. The first boat then gets ahead.

Open Water

As we sail onto open water, the Bay stretches out in every direction; everywhere you look you see water. Water is the Bay region's most precious natural resource. As the skipjack rises and falls over the heaving waters, the boat picks up speed and water sprays on your face. If you lick your lips you notice that the water is slightly salty.

The water in the Chesapeake Bay, like water all over Earth, continually moves from ground to air and back again. This is called the **water cycle.** Energy from the sun heats water and changes it from a liquid to water vapor, a gas. This change is called evaporation. Water vapor rises into the air, then cools and condenses into tiny drops of water that form clouds. Condensation is the change from a gas to a liquid. Rain falls from clouds to Earth's surface.

Water vapor cools and condenses, forming clouds.

Heat from the sun causes evaporation.

Rain or other forms of precipitation fall back to Earth, replenishing the water of the Bay.

This photo is an aerial view of part of the Chesapeake Bay and its many marshes.

The Chesapeake Bay is the largest **estuary** in the United States. An estuary is a place where a river widens out and meets a larger body of water. Water enters the Bay from huge rivers such as the Susquehanna, Potomac, Rappahannock, and James. These and other rivers and streams bring fresh water to the Bay. The Bay then connects with the Atlantic Ocean, where the water is salty.

Water is fresh in and near the streams and rivers of the Chesapeake Bay. It is salty near the mouth where water meets and flows to the Atlantic Ocean. Where fresh and salt water meet in the Bay, the water is **brackish**— a mixture of salt and fresh water. Most water in the Bay is brackish.

∧ Water provides many opportunities for transportation and recreation. Kayaks are common in the Bay and marshes.

Along the Shore

As the skipjack crosses the Bay toward the western shore, you will see an amazing sight—a vast expanse of marsh grass. Here cordgrass and cattails crowd in dense clusters along the shoreline. Marshes are wetlands that are flooded by the tide each day. The Bay's marshland is important to wildlife, providing food and protection for many fish and bird species.

∨ Eelgrass is an important species of aquatic plants. Bay wildlife rely on it for their habitat.

As the skipjack draws close to the shore, the captain needs to be careful not to run aground. As you near shore, look over the side; you will be surprised to see grass growing under the water! It is eelgrass, an aquatic plant that can grow underwater. Eelgrass and other aquatic plants offer important habitats for fish, crabs, and shellfish.

Further along, as the skipjack passes a wooded shore, you'll notice the faint scents of cedar and pine mingling in the moist air. Long ago, the tall, straight pines were valued as ships' masts. Today, some of the trees are still harvested for use as construction lumber or for making paper.

Let's turn the boat around and head back to port.

The best time to see the forest is during autumn. The leaves of oak, beech, and sassafras trees change. They turn amazing shades of yellow, orange, and red.

Sailing Home

As the wind picks up and the skipjack surges back toward port, you can't help noticing the wildlife all around. Flocks of geese honk overhead as they fly in a V formation. Geese and other waterfowl flock to the Bay to spend the winter. Other birds, such as great blue herons and ospreys, stay year round. If you're lucky enough, you'll be able to spot white-tailed deer, raccoons, and other wildlife on the shore. The animals don't seem to fear the boat. Perhaps they know you're only sight seeing.

In the early 1600s, explorers said oysters "lay as thick as stones" in the Chesapeake. Today, hauls of oysters can still be dredged from the bay. But the catch is much smaller.

Pelicans nest on the shore of the Chesapeake.

What other wildlife is here? If you look down under the water, you'll see more. The Bay is home to many species of fish and shellfish. Striped bass, bluefish, oysters, clams, and blue crabs are just a few of the local favorites. Most residents fish for these local delicacies and many restaurants serve fresh fish and shellfish to visitors.

As the skipjack gently pulls into port, you reflect on your sail around the Chesapeake Bay. You think about how the air, water, plants, animals, and other natural resources make the Bay such a wonderful place to visit and live.

Many species of fish live in or visit the Bay's waters, including the oyster toadfish. They are attracted by the rich food supply in the Bay.

Check In What are some of the resources of the Bay?

Saving the Bay

by Barbara Keeler

Captain John Smith was the first English explorer to sail the Chesapeake Bay in the early 1600s. During his exploration of the region he was amazed at the rich **natural resources** the Bay offered. For today's explorers, Smith's *"faire Bay,"* as he referred to the Chesapeake, is different. Like a huge, powerful magnet, the Chesapeake has attracted millions of people. Since Smith's exploration, the population of the Chesapeake region has grown to more than 16 million people. The increased population and the way people live have threatened the natural beauty and resources of the Bay. But people are now working to protect and save the Chesapeake through their **conservation** efforts.

One organization that has led the charge to "Save the Bay" is the Chesapeake Bay Foundation (CBF). From it's beginning in the 1960s, CBF has pushed for laws to protect the Bay. Once conservation laws are passed, CBF partners with governments, industries, and citizens to put them into practice.

CBF also takes direct action, operating hands-on programs. Volunteers work on **restoration** of what has been lost or damaged. Examples include growing oysters, replanting wetlands, restoring forests, and protecting streams.

Volunteers plant eel grass along the shore of the Chesapeake Bay.

A New Way to Farm

"It works for the environment because it protects the Bay," said Michael Heller, manager of Clagett Farm in Maryland. Heller refers to the sustainable farming practices the Chesapeake Bay Foundation recommends. Clagett Farm, a project of CBF, showcases these practices.

Heller knows that **runoff** from farms is a major cause of pollution. When it rains, water picks up and carries excess nutrients from fertilizers and animal waste. Farm runoff also carries toxic insecticides and weed killers used on farms. Eventually the contaminated rainwater enters streams that then flow into the Bay.

CBF has long called for sustainable farming practices. Recommendations include planting trees and other plants alongside waterways to catch and filter runoff. Reducing the amount of chemicals used on crops also helps. CBF also recommends planting cover crops on bare land to keep soil in place and reduce runoff.

Heller and his workers apply all of these methods. They also feed cattle in pastures, where nutrients from manure soak into the grassy ground. The cattle are moved around so that they do not eat the grass to the ground. This gives the pastures time to grow. CBF is convinced if more farms adopt these methods the amount of pollutants reaching the Bay will be vastly reduced.

Cows graze in a pasture at Clagett Farm.

Bringing Back a Bay Native

"Oysters can be restored and sustainably fished with the right approach," said Tommy Leggett, a Chesapeake Bay Foundation scientist.

In John Smith's day, oysters were among the most abundant seafood resources of the Bay. Unfortunately, overfishing and disease have caused the oyster population to plunge. Oysters aren't just good to eat; they are good for the health of the Bay. Oysters feed by filtering algae from the water. In turn, the oysters also filter out sediment and other pollutants. This helps keep bay waters clear and healthy. Oyster reefs also provide habitats for fish and crabs.

Leggett, his small team, and many volunteers work to restore oyster populations in the Bay. First, local restaurants donate oyster shells. Hard-working volunteers wash the shells and put them into mesh bags. Then they stack the bags of shells in large tanks of water containing microscopic oyster **larvae.**

After a few days, the tiny oysters have attached themselves to the shells. Volunteers then drain the tanks and transfer the shells into baskets. The baskets are taken by boat to the Lafayette and Piankatank rivers. Leggett and CBF volunteers then dump the shells onto oyster reefs. The reefs are protected and off-limits to oyster fishing. Now, thanks in part to these restoration efforts, there is hope for restoring the oysters in the Bay.

∨ CBF volunteers work on an oyster restoration project.

Tommy Leggett holds a group of oysters for display during an oyster restoration project.

Students Helping Oysters

"At Christchurch School we recognize that the native oyster is in trouble in the Chesapeake Bay, and we know we can make a difference," says Will Smiley, a science teacher. Located on the Rappahannock River in Virginia, Christchurch is well-situated to participate in oyster restoration. With help from Tommy Leggett of the Chesapeake Bay Foundation, students have raised more than half a million oysters and put them on oyster reefs near the school.

As the oysters grow, students sort and clean them. The largest oysters are lowered to the bottom of the river in special cages that protect them as they continue growing. Students then monitor the growth of the oysters until they reach about 7.5 cm (3 inches) long. The oysters are then harvested and sold during the fall and winter. Christchurch is a licensed oyster shipper. They sell their oysters under the name "Seahorse Oysters," named for the school's mascot.

The school believes that as students are helping oysters, the oysters are helping the students. Oysters make up a big part of the school's education mission. The school is using the oyster program as a tool for teaching about ecology, economics, history, problem solving, and sustainability.

Students from Christchurch School participate in an oyster restoration project.

Check In   What problems are the Chesapeake Bay Foundation trying to solve?

Crabbing
on the Bay

by Richard Easby

Crab cakes anyone?

This mouth-watering dish from the Chesapeake Bay is famous all over the country. The easy way to make them is to just buy some crabmeat. The harder way, which is more fun, is to go fishing for crabs. Before we show you how to fish for crabs, let's learn a little about what you will be catching. First, where can you find crabs? The blue crab spends time in all of the Bay's habitats during its life. Except at mating season, adult males live in the fresher waters of the Bay. Adult females, however, live in the more salty water coming into the Bay from the ocean.

During mating season, the female releases her hatched **larvae** into salty water near the mouth of the Bay. The larvae, which are different in form from their parents, spend their early lives in the ocean. Then they migrate, or move, to the upper Bay and rivers. Here, the young crabs continue to grow in marshy areas of sea grass. During the winter, blue crabs hibernate in the Bay's deep trenches. In warm weather, they migrate to shallow water.

Crabs have paddle-shaped rear legs for swimming.

A crab's shell cannot grow. As a crab grows larger, it must molt, or shed its shell.

Crabs have three pairs of legs for walking.

jimmy

A male crab is called a jimmy. It has a sharply tapered abdomen.

she-crab

An immature female crab is called a she-crab. It has a triangular abdomen.

sook

A mature female crab is called a sook. It has a broad, rounded abdomen.

sponge crab

A female crab with eggs is called a sponge crab. It is named for the egg mass, which is called a sponge.

What You Will Need

There are many ways to catch crabs, but the most fun is to use a drop line or a net. This way you will catch one crab at a time. You may not catch a large number of crabs in the Chesapeake, but you can catch enough to eat if you go about it correctly. To start, you need to gather all the tools and materials you will need.

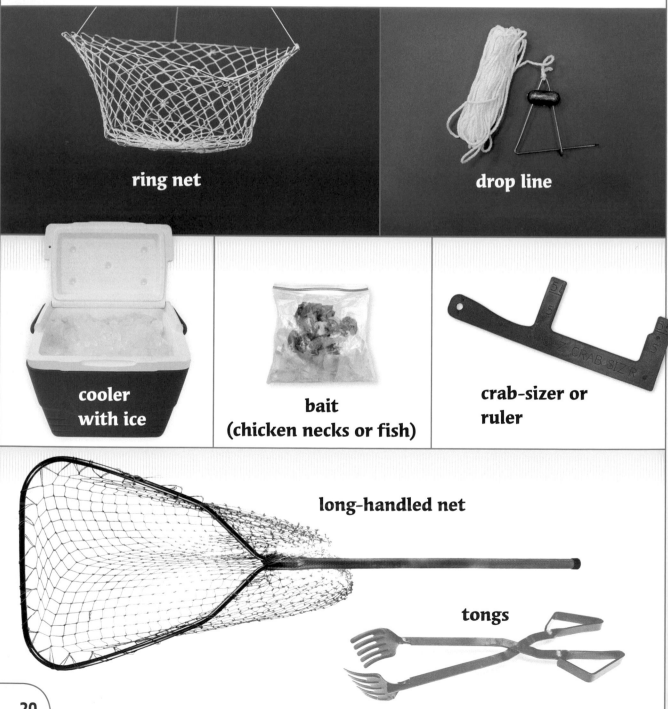

ring net

drop line

cooler with ice

bait
(chicken necks or fish)

crab-sizer or ruler

long-handled net

tongs

1. Find a good spot.

First, you will need to choose your crabbing place. You can drop your line in from a public fishing pier or a bridge. Ask the locals where the best places are. You can also fish for crabs from a boat.

2. Bait your net.

Next, tie your bait to your line or fasten it to the bottom of your ring net. Chicken necks are a good choice for bait because they are meaty enough to attract crabs and boney enough to prevent the crab from quickly tearing them to pieces.

3. Drop in your net.

Next, drop your baited line or net into the water. Either hold onto the line or tie it to the dock or pier. When you feel or see the line move, a crab may be eating the bait. Pull the line in extremely slowly. Don't get frustrated if the crab drops off. This happens often when you are crabbing with a line. Just throw the line back into the water and start again.

If you are using a ring net, you may not know if a crab is eating the bait. It is best to wait 15 minutes, then quickly pull the net in to see if you have caught a crab.

4. Land a crab.

If you have a crab on a line, you will also need to have your long-handled net ready. It is easier to have another person help you with the net. Lower the net into the water only after the crab is seen. Try to avoid accidentally hitting the crab with the net, which may cause the crab to let go and swim away. Be very careful, because crabs get spooked by noise or if you pull the line too fast. If all goes well, scoop the crab into the net and place it into the cooler. Measure to make sure your crab is legal size. You will need to check the local fishing regulations wherever you're crabbing for the size and type you can keep.

Crab Cake Recipe

Once you have your crabs, you will want to eat them. Here is a traditional recipe for crab cakes. As one Chesapeake Bay resident said, "Growing up near the Chesapeake Bay, you learn that crabs are as valuable as gold. I've been making crab cakes since I was old enough to reach the kitchen counter."

Ingredients

450 grams (about one pound) of crabmeat

*⅓ cup crushed crackers

3 green onions, finely chopped

½ cup chopped red bell pepper

½ lemon, juiced

1 egg, beaten

¼ cup mayonnaise

1 teaspoon Dijon-style prepared mustard

1 teaspoon Worcestershire sauce

1 teaspoon salt

⅓ cup vegetable or olive oil

5-Step Directions

1. Pick through the crabmeat to remove pieces of shell.

2. Break the crackers into small pieces and place in a medium-size bowl with crabmeat. Add onions, pepper, lemon juice, egg, mayonnaise, mustard, Worcestershire sauce, and salt.

3. Mix ingredients by hand. Don't overwork the crabmeat. Keep the meat in lumps as much as possible.

4. Form the mixture into about 6 patties.

5. Heat the oil in a skillet over medium heat. When the oil is hot, carefully add crab cakes. Fry them two at a time. Fry for 4–5 minutes until they are golden brown. Carefully flip them. Cook for another 4 minutes until golden brown.

*You can make this recipe gluten free by using gluten-free crackers.

Check In What are the steps in catching crabs?

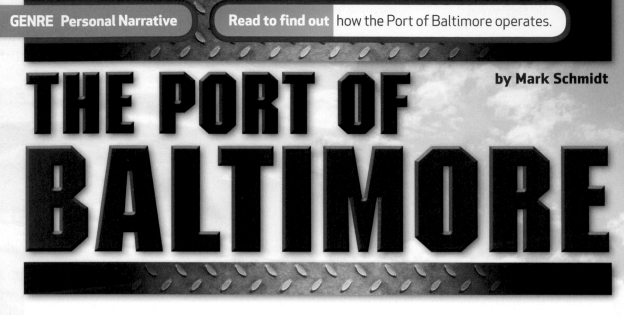

Read to find out how the Port of Baltimore operates.

by Mark Schmidt

THE PORT OF BALTIMORE

Mark Schmidt, Terminal Manager, Facility Ports America Chesapeake

Hello and welcome to the Port of Baltimore! My name is Mark Schmidt. I work here at the Port. It's one of the busiest shipping places in the Chesapeake Bay region. Ships from all over the world dock here. Then cargo containing all sorts of resources, such as coal and steel, and even cars, are loaded or unloaded at the docks. It's a constant movement of machines, people, and goods. Let me tell you more about what I mean and share with you more about my job.

You see, I like to watch it all happen. In fact, it's my job! I watch all the goings-on using a pair of binoculars I keep in my office. My office, right on the water's edge, has the best view of the harbor.

I watch the entire shipping process as each ship comes into port, is docked, unloaded, reloaded, and then leaves. Each cargo ship needs a pilot to help the crew dock, or park. The pilot knows the port very well and ensures each ship is docked safely. A small boat takes the pilot to the incoming ship.

The docking pilot steers the ship through the port and into a **berth.** The berth is the area next to shore where a ship docks. At the Seagirt Marine Terminal, which I manage, even the largest ships can dock. It's an amazing sight to watch! We have a new 15-meter (50-feet) deep berth. It is one of only two in the eastern United States. So we can accept some very large ships and a lot of cargo.

The Port of Baltimore is in Baltimore, Maryland. The Chesapeake Bay is the water route to and from the Atlantic Ocean.

A ship is docked at a terminal berth. The terminal's gigantic cranes load and unload shipping containers.

Seagirt Marine Terminal handles container ships which carry huge metal containers full of goods. They are so big that old containers can be turned into homes. To lift them, we need gigantic cranes. Some of our newer cranes are as high as a 14-story building.

The cranes are so tall that they barely fit under some of the largest bridges. When the cranes were first delivered for installation, I rode on the top of one. I just climbed up for the view, which was even better than the view from my office!

The work continues as dock workers load the cargo directly onto trucks and railcars. The crane's monstrous steel claw easily plucks 12-meter (40-foot) containers from the ship's deck and loads them onto flatbed trucks. Sitting in cabs 45 meters (150 feet) high, workers operate the crane as it lifts and lowers each giant metal box.

Once loaded, the trucks and trains can begin their deliveries. Because of the Port's location, cargo can be delivered within 24 hours to about 35 percent of America's factories and 32 percent of its population.

Once a ship is unloaded, trucks line up three-deep with containers of goods ready to be loaded onto the ship and moved out of the port. They may contain **natural resources** such as lumber or corn and soybeans from Chesapeake Bay farms.

The cranes load the containers from the trucks to the ship, stacking one on top of the other. The pilot then boards the ship and guides it out into the Bay. There, another pilot who knows the Chesapeake Bay well guides the ship to the ocean. Then the ship's captain takes over and guides the ship across the ocean, perhaps to another continent.

I hope you enjoyed this snapshot of how the Port of Baltimore works and how important the Chesapeake Bay is to moving cargo throughout the region.

Cranes move containers from a ship to waiting trucks.

Check In What is important about the location of the Port of Baltimore?

Discuss

1. What Chesapeake Bay resources did you learn about in each selection? How are these resources used?

2. Is your home environment similar to the Chesapeake Bay or very different? What resources do you have where you live?

3. Discuss with a partner what is being done to save the Bay. What efforts do you know about in your own community to help the local environment?

4. What questions would you ask Mark Schmidt about his work at the Port of Baltimore? How could you find answers to some of these questions?

5. What do you still wonder about the Chesapeake Bay? How could you learn more?